Complete the Code

Student Workbook

William Collins' dream of knowledge for all began with the publication of his first book in 1819.
A self-educated mill worker, he not only enriched millions of lives, but also founded a flourishing publishing house.
Today, staying true to this spirit, Collins books are packed with inspiration, innovation and practical expertise.
They place you at the centre of a world of possibility and give you exactly what you need to explore it.

Published by Collins
An imprint of HarperCollins*Publishers*
The News Building, 1 London Bridge Street, London, SE1 9GF, UK

HarperCollins*Publishers*
Macken House, 39/40 Mayor Street Upper, Dublin 1, D01 C9W8, Ireland

Browse the complete Collins catalogue at
collins.co.uk

© Wandle Learning Trust 2026
littlewandlecode.org.uk

10 9 8 7 6 5 4 3 2 1

A catalogue record for this publication is available from the British Library.

ISBN 978-0-00-879104-9

All rights reserved. No part of this publication may be reproduced, stored in a retrieval system, or transmitted in any form by any means, electronic, mechanical, photocopying, recording or otherwise, without the prior written permission of the Publisher or a licence permitting restricted copying in the United Kingdom issued by the Copyright Licensing Agency Ltd, 5th Floor, Shackleton House, 4 Battle Bridge Lane, London SE1 2HX.

Without limiting the exclusive rights of any author, contributor or the publisher of this publication, any unauthorised use of this publication to train generative artificial intelligence (AI) technologies is expressly prohibited. HarperCollins also exercise their rights under Article 4(3) of the Digital Single Market Directive 2019/790 and expressly reserve this publication from the text and data mining exception.

Little Wandle Code has been developed by
Wandle Learning Trust in collaboration with Collins.

At Wandle Learning Trust:
Author: Sarah Paxton
Project manager: Rachel Russ
Editors: Helen Lawson, Caroline Hale, Tracy Kewley
Proofreaders: Jane Jackson, Jennie Clifford
Cover designer: Communitas
Internal designers and typesetters: Communitas, Tech-Set

At Collins:
Publisher: Katie Sergeant
Product manager: Natasha Paul
Production controller: Sophie Waeland

Printed in the UK

Acknowledgements

The publishers gratefully acknowledge the permission granted to reproduce the copyright material in this book. Every effort has been made to trace copyright holders and to obtain their permission for the use of copyright material. The publishers will gladly receive any information enabling them to rectify any error or omission at the first opportunity.

Mnemonic illustrations by Noah Warnes
Other illustrations by Marek Jagucki,
apart from p. 9: New Vectors/Shutterstock

Contents

Unit 1 (Sessions 1.1 to 1.4)	5
Unit 2 (Sessions 2.1 to 2.4)	11
Unit 3 (Sessions 3.1 to 3.4)	17
Unit 4 (Sessions 4.1 to 4.4)	23
Unit 5 (Sessions 5.1 to 5.4)	29
Unit 6 (Sessions 6.1 to 6.4)	35
Unit 7 (Sessions 7.1 to 7.4)	41
Unit 8 (Sessions 8.1 to 8.4)	47
Unit 9 (Sessions 9.1 to 9.4)	53
Unit 10 (Sessions 10.1 to 10.4)	59
Unit 11 (Sessions 11.1 to 11.4)	65
Unit 12 (Sessions 12.1 to 12.4)	71
Unit 13 (Sessions 13.1 to 13.4)	77
Unit 14 (Sessions 14.1 to 14.4)	83
Complete the Code Chart	94
Glossary	96

Session 1.1

Table 1

	👆	✏️
sun	3	sun
zip		
splat		
laptop		

Table 2

	👆	✏️
soak		
seed		
chair		
airtight		
shape		

Session 1.2
Code Review

Consonants

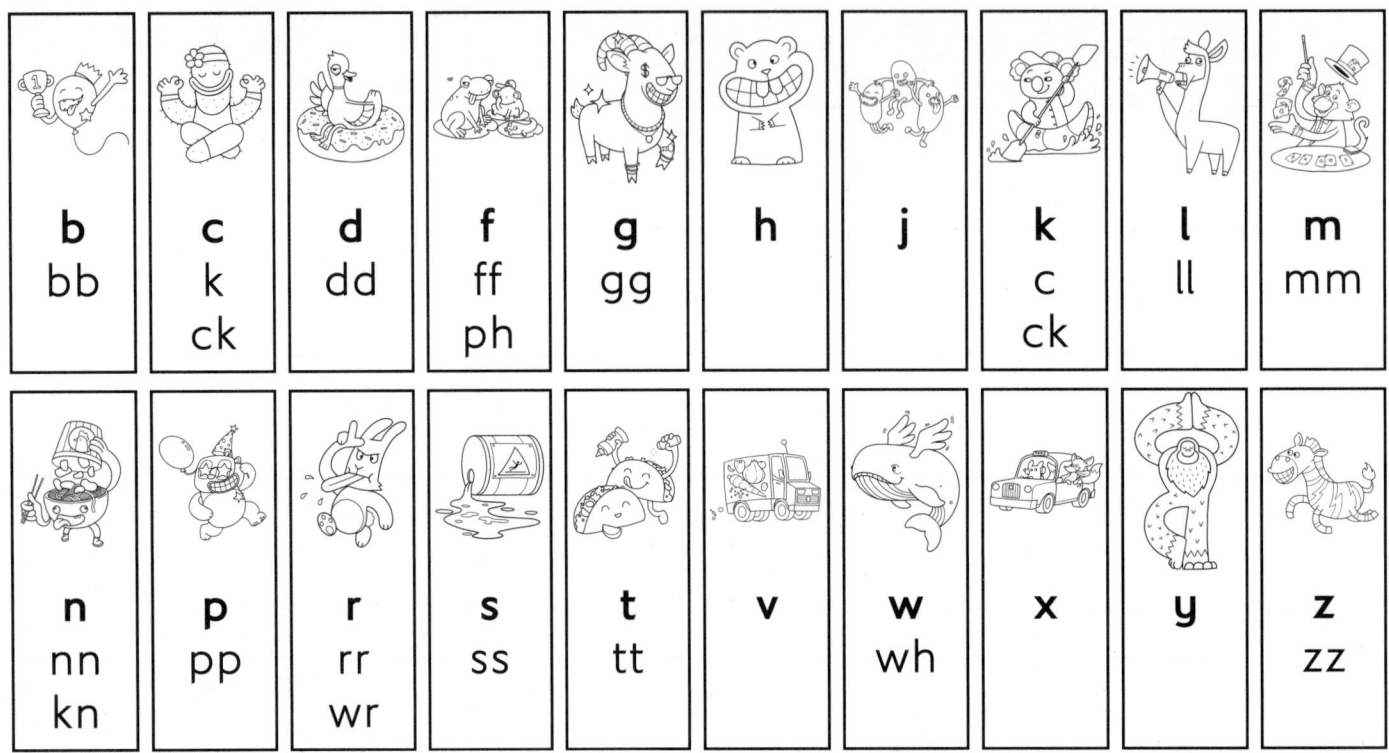

Consonant Digraphs

*This has a slight schwa at the end, 'chuh'.

Vowels

a   e   i   o   u

Vowel Digraphs and Trigraphs

  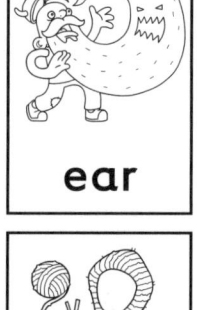    

ai   air   ar   ear   ee   er   igh

oa   oi   oo   oo   or   ow   ur

Session 1.3

Table 1

	👏
bucket	2
street	
highlight	
magnetic	
helicopter	

Table 2

	👏	Prefix	Word	Suffix
brighter	2		bright	er
frowning				
unafraid				
development				
disrespectful				

Session 1.4
You as a Reader

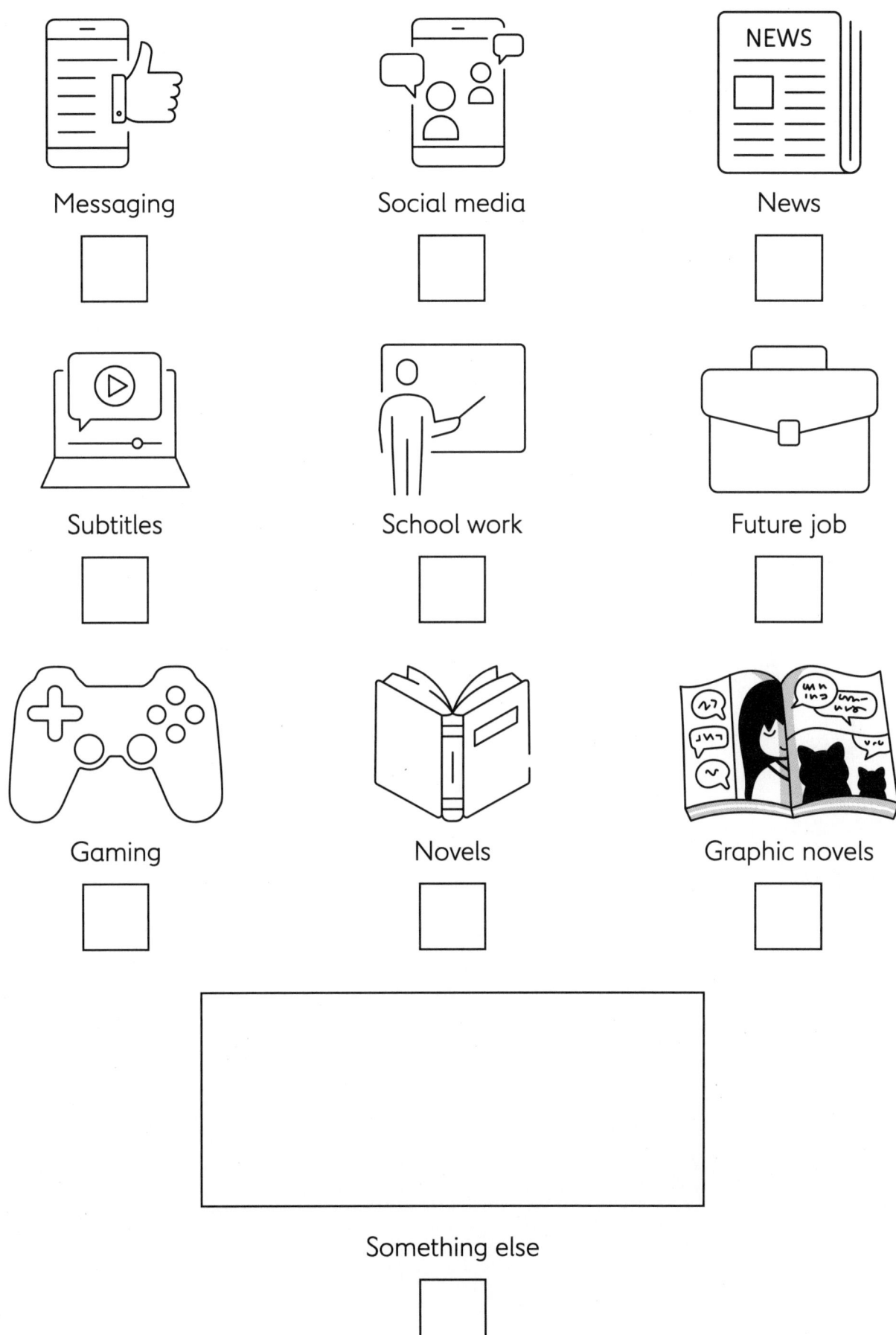

Messaging ☐

Social media ☐

News ☐

Subtitles ☐

School work ☐

Future job ☐

Gaming ☐

Novels ☐

Graphic novels ☐

Something else ☐

Code Agreement

I agree to:

- Follow instructions

- Listen to my teacher

- Be kind to my peers

- Not give up, even when it is hard

- Remember that mistakes help me learn

- Ask for help if I need it

- Take my reading learning seriously.

Signed _____

Session 2.1 /ai/ a-e, ai

Map it

air	n	oo	ow
w	wr	kn	ear
r	oi	wh	ee

Learn New Code

a-e	ai
make	rain
'a-e' is the most common spelling in the middle of a word.	'ai' is usually in the middle of a word.

Spell it: Add it

Word	Suffix	New Word	
estimate		estimated	4
inflate	ed		
animate			
translate			
pollinate			

Summary

a-e	ai
make	rain
estimate	explain
translate	sprain
pollinate	contain
inflate	
animate	

Session 2.2 /ai/ ay, a

Map it

ch	wr	tch	oo
ee	oa	a-e	oi
ai	zz	wh	air

Learn New Code

ay	a
play	wafer
'ay' is usually at the end of words or syllables.	'a' is often the second grapheme in a word.

Spell it: Add it

Word	Suffix	New Word	👆
decay	ed	decayed	2
play			
betray			
display			
pray			

Summary

ay	a
play	wafer
decay	crater
essay	major
layer	data
decayed	
played	
betrayed	
displayed	
prayed	

Session 2.4

Code it

contain	decay	frustrate
display	brave	waist
explain	crater	paper
layer	holiday	translate
blame	acorn	spray
major	essay	afraid
pollinate	bagel	basic
train	update	snail
painting	apron	estimate
operate	entertain	dismay

Make it

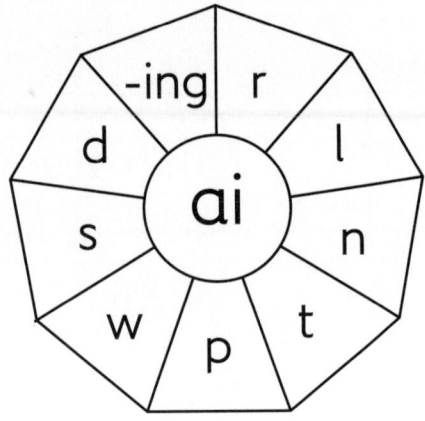

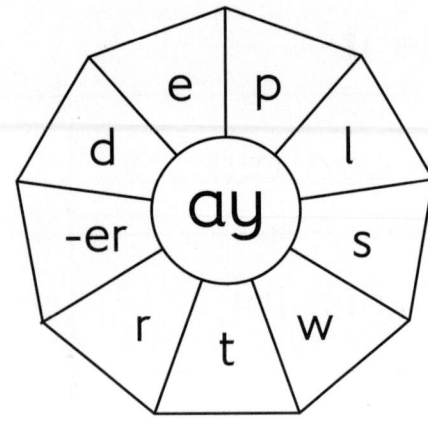

Hints:
1. To travel on a ship.
2. An animal that's like a slug with a shell.
3. If something hurts, you are in ____.

Hints:
1. To take part in a match.
2. 24 hours.
3. To not move.

Session 3.1 /j/ g, ge, dge

Map it

ai	ee	a-e	ow
kn	oi	oo	ay
n	ear	a	igh

Learn New Code

g	ge	dge
gem	large	badge
'g' is always found at the beginning or in the middle of a word.	'ge' is usually found at the end of a word.	'dge' is usually found at the end of a word.

Spell it: Add it

Word	Suffix	New Word	
judge		judgement	2
pay			
develop	ment		
equip			
state			

Summary

g	ge	dge
gem digit allergic	large dungeon average	badge edge judge judgement

Session 3.2 /s/ c, ce, sc

Map it

g	a-e	air	ai
oa	dge	a	ge
ay	oi	j	igh

Learn New Code

c	ce	sc
cell	voice	scent
'c' never appears at the end of a word.	'ce' is usually found at the end of a word.	'sc' is an unusual spelling. It appears at the beginning or in the middle of a word.

Spell it: Add it

Word	Suffix	New Word	
celebrate		celebrating	4
translate	ing		
estimate			
pollinate			
demonstrate			

Summary

c	ce	sc
cell acidic celebrate celebrating	surface voice evidence	scent muscle adolescent

Session 3.4

Code it

average	cinnamon	challenge
surface	sledge	digit
dungeon	celebrate	service
bridge	adolescent	evidence
citrus	allergic	bandage
sentence	muscle	concentrate
fascinate	grudge	register
legend	scissors	justice
pencil	exchange	gerbil
judge	scent	fudge

Make it

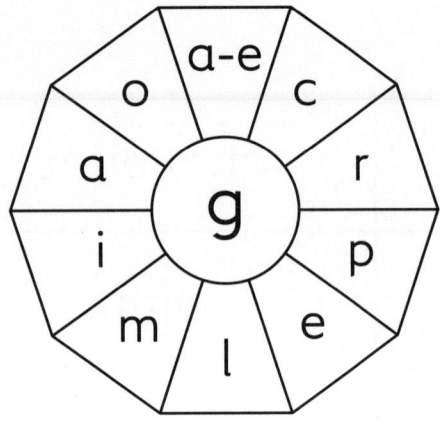

Hints:
1. You keep a pet hamster in this.
2. _____ = anger
3. The number of years since you were born is your _____.

Hints:
1. The planets are in this place.
2. She ran to win the _____.
3. I have a _____ on my teeth.

Session 4.1 /ee/ y, ea, ee

Map it

dge	wh	s	ee
c	sc	g	ch
ge	ce	w	tch

Learn New Code

y	ea	ee
empty	leaf	speech
'y' is the most common way to spell /ee/. It always appears at the end of a word.	'ea' often appears in the middle of a word.	'ee' often appears in the middle of a word.

Spell it: Add it

Word	Suffix	New Word	
factory		factories	3
galaxy			
body	es		
family			
allergy			

Summary

y	ea	ee
empty	leaf	speech
galaxy	season	agree
factory	reason	referee
body		
family		
allergy		

Session 4.2 /ee/ e, ie, e-e

Map it

a-e	sc	c	ee
ce	a	y	ai
r	s	ay	wr

Learn New Code

e	ie	e-e
lemur	field	meme
'e' always appears at the end of a one-syllable word. It usually appears in the middle of a word with more than one syllable.	'ie' always appears in the middle or at the end of a word.	'e-e' is the least common way of spelling /ee/. The most common word with 'e-e' is 'these'.

Spell it: Add it

Word	Suffix	New Word	
achieve	ment	achievement	3
agree			
amaze			
adjust			
refresh			

Summary

e	ie	e-e
lemur simile create	field belief achieve achievement	meme athlete extreme

Session 4.4

Code it

streamer	galaxy	reading
agree	simile	shriek
season	windscreen	vegan
detox	create	comedy
factory	achieve	teacher
believe	greedy	extreme
squeaky	athlete	ability
compete	thief	referee
charity	centipede	married
weekend	recipe	stampede

Make it

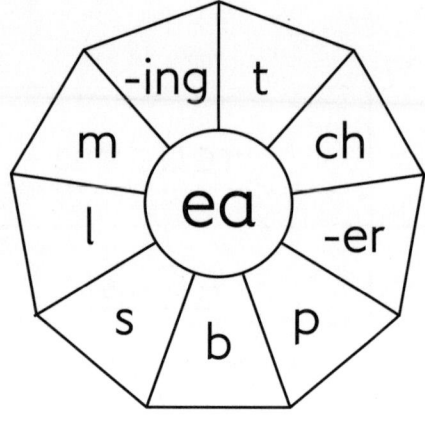
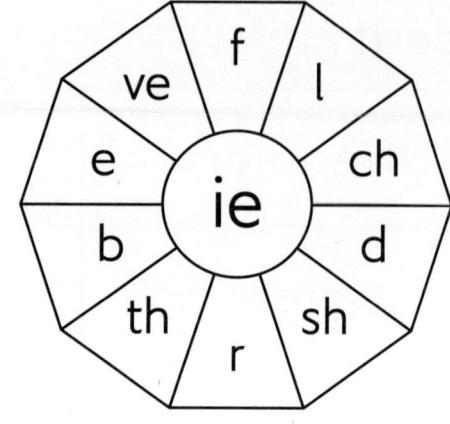

Hints:
1. Not costing much.
2. A thing you sit on.
3. _____ = jump

Hints:
1. A big bit of land for animals like sheep.
2. I sighed with _____ after the test had ended.
3. Someone who steals something.

Session 5.1 /igh/ igh, i-e, i

Map it

y	e-e	oo	air
ow	ie	sh	ea
oi	ee	e	or

Learn New Code

igh	i-e	i
night	like	find
'igh' usually appears in the middle of a word.	'i-e' almost always appears in the middle of a word.	'i' usually appears in the middle of a word.

Spell it: Add it

Word	Suffix	New Word	
environment		environmental	5
digit	al		
logic			
judgement			
person			

Summary

igh	i-e	i
night highlight frightening	like define precise	find climate environment environmental

Session 5.2 /igh/ y, ie

Map it

e	i-e	igh	dge
ee	j	wh	w
i	g	e-e	ge

Learn New Code

y	ie
by	pie
When the /igh/ phoneme is at the end of a word, it is almost always spelled 'y'.	'ie' only appears in the middle or at the end of a word.

Spell it: Lookalikes

/igh/	/ee/

Summary

y	ie
by analyse magnify cyber	pie identified horrified simplified tried applied

Session 5.4

Code it

classified	magnify	divide
analyse	denied	frightening
applied	sublime	magnified
streetlight	cyber	dandelion
environment	highlight	identified
simplify	vibrate	hydrate
enlighten	comply	excitement
precise	bypass	tyrant
horrified	climate	triangle
sunshine	satisfied	slightly

Make it

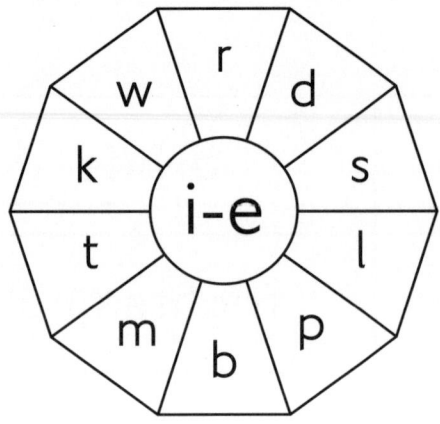 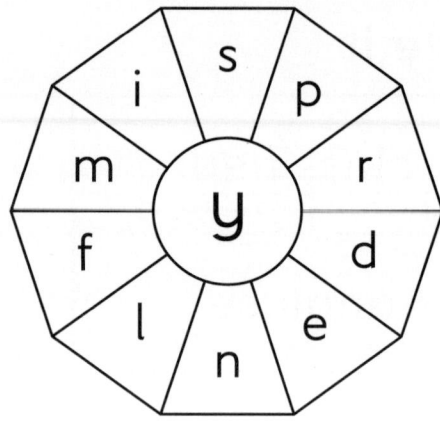

Hints:
1. _____ = grin
2. A woman on her wedding day.
3. The name for a pack of lions.
4. _____ = clever/like an owl

Hints:
1. The opposite of wet.
2. You need wings to do this.
3. To cook in oil.
4. When you respond to something, you _____.

Session 6.1 /oa/ ow, o

Map it

ay	sc	y	a
ie	igh	i	a-e
i-e	ce	ai	c

Learn New Code

ow	o
grow	no
'ow' always appears at the end of a word.	'o' can appear anywhere in a word.

Spell it: Lookalikes

/ow/	/oa/

Summary

ow	o
grow	no
overthrow	tempo
shadow	cytoplasm
shallow	poetry
thrown	
window	

Session 6.2 /oa/ o-e, oa

Map it

ear	e	oa	ee
ea	o	ow	e-e
ie	y	wr	oi

Learn New Code

o-e	oa
home	boat
'o-e' is only used in the middle of a word.	'oa' is usually in the middle of a word.

Spell it: Add it

Word	Suffix	New Word	
boast		boastful	2
forget			
faith	ful		
success			
thank			

Summary

o-e	oa
home ozone compose erode	boat boast overload hoax boastful

Session 6.4

Code it

backbone	shallow	tempo
boast	ozone	throwing
hollow	homesick	overload
limestone	clothing	window
retro	approach	cyclone
compose	overthrow	raincoat
poetry	roadside	buffalo
postcode	lifeboat	cytoplasm
bungalow	locate	owner
bonus	bloated	erode

Make it

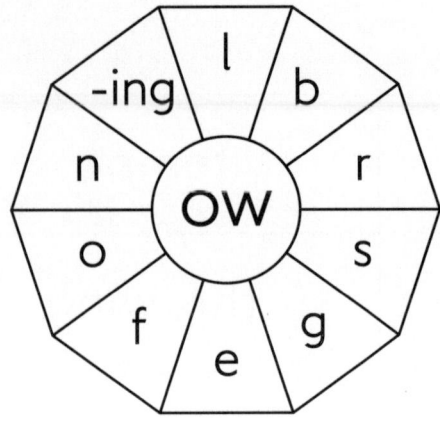 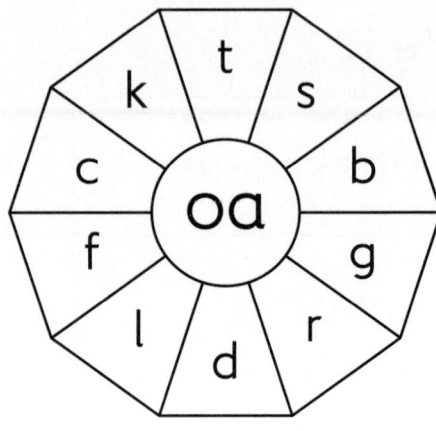

Hints:
1. _____ = not fast
2. _____ = not high
3. The part of your body that joins your upper arm to your lower arm.
4. To shine a little.

Hints:
1. A baby horse.
2. Which tree do acorns come from?
3. The noise a frog makes.
4. To drench in water.

Session 7.1 /oo/, /yoo/ oo, u, ew

Map it

ow	a-e	ay	ie
i-e	o	i	igh
o-e	y	a	oa

Learn New Code

oo	u	ew
soon	flu	chew
'oo' is usually in the middle of a word.	'u' can appear anywhere in a word. When /yoo/ is at the beginning of a word, it is usually spelled 'u'.	'ew' is usually at the end of a word.

Spell it: Add it

Word	Suffix	New Word	
accurate	ly	accurately	4
precise			
extreme			
smooth			
quick			

Summary

oo	u	ew
soon monsoon smooth smoothly	flu fluid accurate accurately	chew newborn renewable

Session 7.2 /oo/, /yoo/ u-e, ue

Map it

ea	oo	e	oa
u	e-e	ee	y
ow	ew	ie	ay

Learn New Code

u-e	ue
tune	blue
'u-e' is almost always in the middle of a word.	'ue' is always at the end of a word, unless it is a compound word.

Spell it: Add it

Word	Suffix	New Word	👆
value	able	valuable	3
achieve			
believe			
debate			
excite			

Summary

u-e	ue
tune	blue
attitude	argue
dilute	value
pollute	continue

Session 7.4

Code it

perfume	fluid	fewest
smooth	dilute	volume
argue	revenue	renewable
toothbrush	reduce	educate
newborn	overdue	pollute
attitude	accurate	classroom
monsoon	continue	distribute
gluten	rescue	chewing
gluepot	cashew	toolbox
costume	statue	communicate

Make it

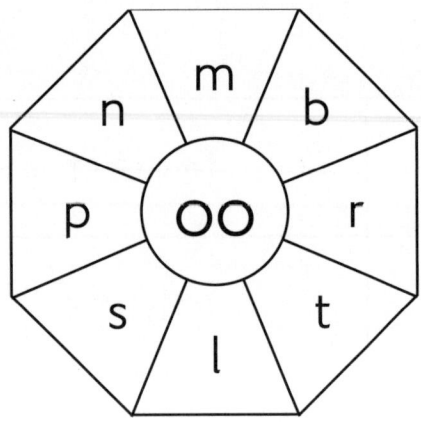

_____

_____

_____

_____

_____

_____

_____

_____

Hints:
1. It is in the sky at night.
2. You sleep in your bed_____.
3. You might swim in a _____.
4. The noise a cow makes.

Hints:
1. April, May, _____
2. _____ = not polite
3. At school, you follow the _____.

Session 8.1 /ow/ ou, ow

Map it

ie	ai	i	ew
u-e	i-e	a	ue
igh	u	oo	y

Learn New Code

ou	ow
out	how
'ou' is always at the beginning or in the middle of a word.	'ow' is usually in the middle or at the end of a word.

Spell it: Lookalikes

/ow/	/oa/

Summary

ou	ow
out	how
mountain	download
county	vowel
surround	browse
	crowded
	frowning

Session 8.2 /oi/ oi, oy

Map it

ow	ge	ie	j
ou	ee	dge	ea
y	e-e	e	g

Learn New Code

oi	oy
boil	boy
'oi' is used at the beginning or in the middle of a word.	'oy' usually appears at the end of a word.

Spell it: Add it

Word	Suffix	New Word	
poison	ous	poisonous	3
mountain			
hazard			
danger			
scandal			

Summary

oi	oy
boil	boy
poison	destroy
disappoint	voyage
exploit	employ
poisonous	

Session 8.4

Code it

nightgown	poison	vowel
asteroid	surround	avoid
counter	destroy	shower
browse	voyage	however
disappoint	mouth	cowboy
powder	annoy	account
mountain	joint	exploit
brownie	employ	joyful
without	choice	countdown
oyster	download	royal

Make it

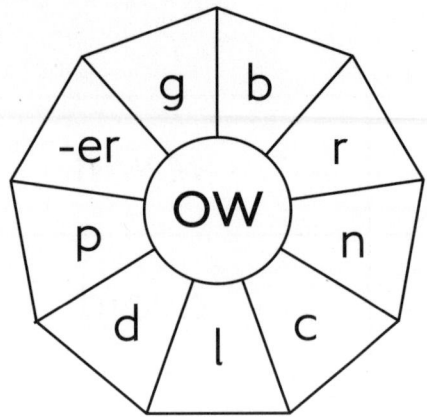
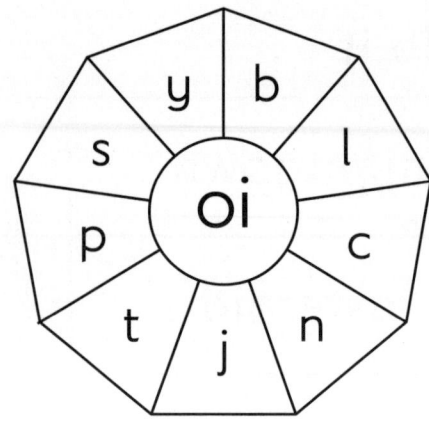

Hints:
1. The animal that says "twit twoo".
2. _____ = not up
3. A king or queen has one of these.
4. An animal that makes milk.

Hints:
1. _____ = loud
2. You can fry things in this liquid.
3. When water is heated, it _____.
4. Your hip, knee and elbows are _____.

Session 9.1 /e/ e, ea

Map it

ng	oy	ow	ee
oi	e-e	ou	sh
e	nk	y	ie

Learn New Code

e	ea
index	bread
'e' is the most common way to spell /e/.	When /e/ is spelled 'ea', it always appears in the middle of a word.

Spell it: Lookalikes

/e/	/ee/

Summary

e	ea
index extinct method ethical	bread heaven wealthy weather ready feather

Session 9.2 /i/ i, y

Map it

i-e	u-e	u	i
ew	ea	oi	oo
oy	ue	ie	e

Learn New Code

i	y
import	gym
'i' is the most common way to spell /i/.	When /i/ is spelled 'y', it always appears in the middle of a word.

Spell it: Add it

Prefix	Word	New Word	👆
mis	inform	misinform	3
	interpret		
	behave		
	trust		
	understand		

Summary

i	y
import abolish invade inform interpret misinform misinterpret	gym myth syllable ecosystem

Session 9.4

Code it

gym	breakfast	cobweb
syrup	sketch	wealth
instead	cymbal	pyramid
crystal	mystery	thread
health	meadow	symbol
myth	dread	squishy
syllable	weapon	cryptic
peasant	tread	symptom
crypt	stealth	chicken
threat	typical	breath

Make it

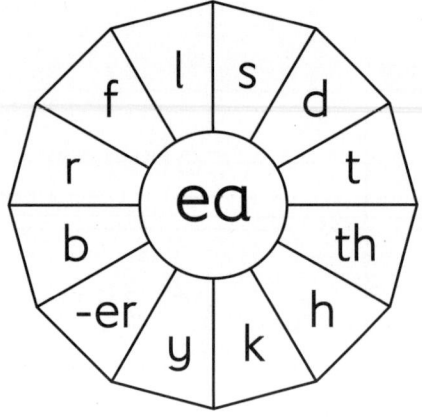 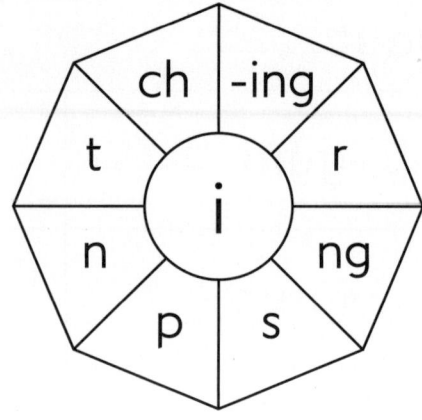

_____   _____

_____   _____

_____   _____

_____   _____

_____   _____

_____   _____

_____   _____

Hints:
1. _____, steady, go!
2. The part of your body that your brain is inside.
3. Someone who is unable to hear is _____.

Hints:
1. Fish and _____.
2. Very wealthy.
3. Drink a little bit.
4. Your phone _____ when someone calls.

58

Session 10.1 /o/ o, a

Map it

ay	or	i	a
y	e	air	a-e
ea	ou	ow	ai

Learn New Code

o	a
frost	want
'o' is the most common way to spell /o/.	'a' is an unusual way to spell /o/. It often follows 'w' or 'qu'.

Spell it: Add it

Prefix	Word	New Word	👏
in	equality	inequality	5
	accurate		
	correct		
	flexible		
	visible		

Summary

o	a
frost economy hypothesis contribute correct incorrect	want equality alter quantity inequality

Session 10.2 /u/ u, o, ou

Map it

tch	o	sc	ow
a	oy	ch	c
ea	ce	oi	ou

Learn New Code

u	o	ou
under	front	young
'u' is the most common way to spell /u/.	When /u/ is spelled 'o', it always appears in the middle of a word.	'ou' is an unusual spelling for /u/. It always appears in the middle of a word.

Spell it: Lookalikes

/ow/	/u/

Summary

u	o	ou
under substance summarise	front compass govern	young southern courage double

Session 10.4

Code it

squash	oven	other
country	wander	young
salt	worry	quad
wallet	unstuck	trouble
mother	touch	swamp
comfort	watch	month
double	honey	wasp
squabble	couple	wonder
nothing	swap	nourish
brother	cousin	money

Make it

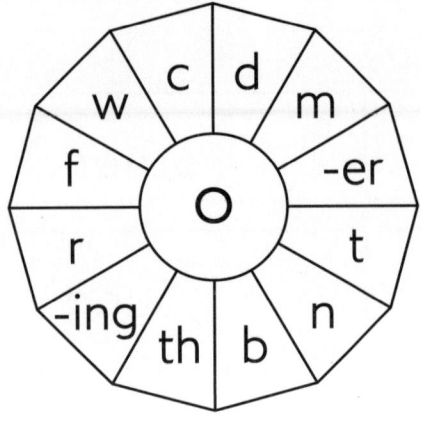

Hints:
1. Your male sibling is your _____.
2. The opposite of back = _____
3. March, April and May are _____s.

Hints:
1. Twice as much = _____
2. Your uncle's son is your _____.
3. Two people can be a _____.

Session 11.1 /or/ or, a, aw

Map it

e-e	u	oi	ie
ng	e	o	ea
ee	oy	y	ou

Learn New Code

or	a	aw
for	water	saw
'or' is the most common way to spell /or/.	When /or/ is spelled 'a', it is often followed by 'l'.	'aw' is usually in the middle or at the end of a word.

Spell it: Add it

Word	Suffix	New Word	👏
law		lawless	2
use			
hope	less		
home			
defence			

Summary

or	a	aw
for	water	saw
order	install	law
afford	appalling	drawbridge
		lawless

Session 11.2 /or/ au, ore

Map it

ea	ou	or	w
a	u	aw	y
o	wh	e	i

Learn New Code

au	ore
haunt	bore
'au' is usually at the beginning or in the middle of a word.	'ore' is usually at the end of a word.

Spell it: Add it

Word	Suffix	New Word	
explore		explorer	3
compose	er		
write			
dance			
manage			

Summary

au	ore
haunt author audience automatic	bore carnivore explore explorer seashore

Session 11.4

Code it

orbit	sawdust	spore
sauce	sporting	almost
haunted	walnut	chores
already	stormy	seesaw
export	ignore	passport
snore	astronaut	prawn
outlaw	launch	always
implore	fraudster	straw
also	jigsaw	authentic
chainsaw	sycamore	popcorn

Make it

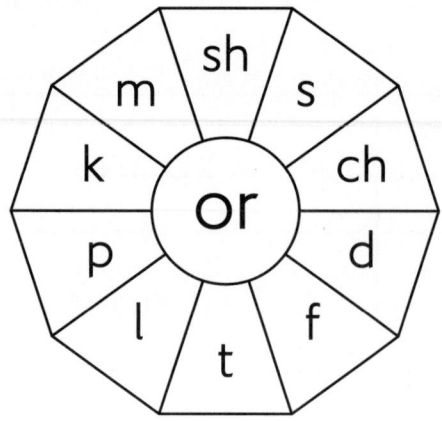

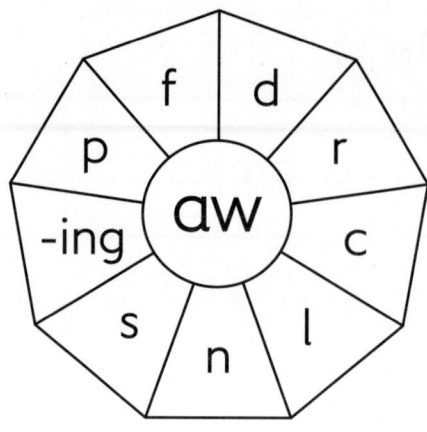

Hints:
1. You eat with a knife and _____.
2. Cut-off trousers.
3. A hand-held light.
4. Football, cricket and basketball are _____.

Hints:
1. Use a pencil to make a picture.
2. A big, mown space of grass.
3. Not cooked.
4. A dog's foot is called a _____.

Session 12.1 /ur/ er, ur

Map it

ear	or	a	o
au	ore	ow	oi
o-e	oy	oa	aw

Learn New Code

er	**ur**
her	turn
'er' is the most common way to spell /ur/.	'ur' is usually in the middle or at the end of a word.

Spell it: Add it

Word	Suffix	New Word	
vertical		vertically	4
environmental	ly		
horizontal			
comical			
accidental			

Summary

er	ur
her vertical vertically adverb iceberg	turn murmur nocturnal hurdle

Session 12.2 /ur/ ir, or

Map it

dge	e	ur	j
y	ea	er	i
u	ge	o	ou

Learn New Code

ir	or
bird	word
'ir' is usually in the middle or at the end of a word.	'or' is an unusual spelling for /ur/. It is usually in the middle of a word.

Spell it: Add it

Prefix	Word	New Word	
out	grow	outgrow	2
	law		
	burst		
	live		
	number		

Summary

ir	or
bird confirm outskirts circumference	word worship bookworm worth

Session 12.4

Code it

disturb	perfect	shirk
worthy	worst	occur
emerge	childbirth	burger
third	work	birdseed
blurb	lurking	world
chirp	external	verb
burst	thirsty	flatworm
expert	church	finger
artwork	number	hurting
proverb	codewords	stern

Make it

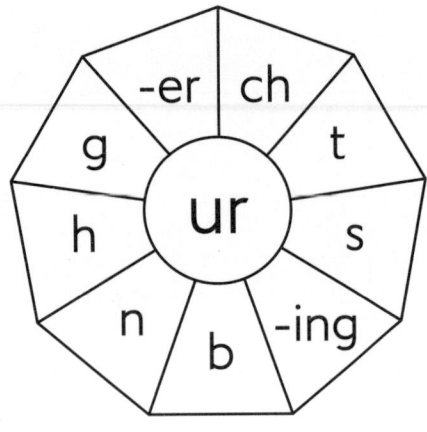 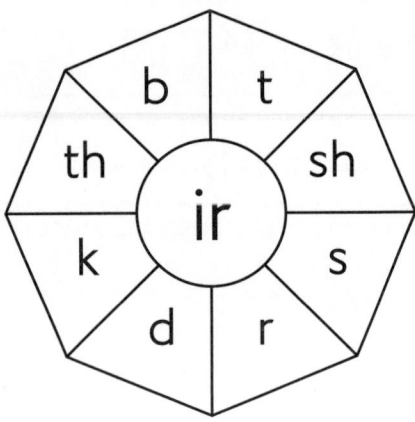

Hints:
1. If you leave your bread in the toaster for too long, it _____.
2. A meat patty in a bun.
3. Pop (a balloon) = _____

Hints:
1. An item of clothing.
2. A flying animal.
3. To mix with a spoon.

Session 13.1 /air/ air, are, ear

Map it

ue	er	ai	ur
ir	u	oo	ay
or	u-e	a-e	ew

Learn New Code

air	are	ear
chair	care	bear
'air' is the most common way to spell /air/.	'are' only appears at the end of a word.	'ear' only appears at the end of a word.

Spell it: Lookalikes

/ear/	/air/

Summary

air	are	ear
chair wheelchair repair	care software compare	bear footwear swear wear tear

Session 13.2 /ear/ ear, er, ere

Map it

ou	a	are	aw
au	ore	ear	ea
u	or	air	o

Learn New Code

ear	**er**	**ere**
hear	hero	here
'ear' usually appears at the end of a word.	'er' always appears in the middle of a word.	'ere' always appears at the end of a word.

Spell it: Add it

Prefix	Word	New Word	👆
dis	appear	disappear	3
	agree		
	appoint		
	connect		
	like		

Summary

ear	er	ere
hear disappear appear fearful	hero bacteria material	here atmosphere persevere

Session 13.4

Code it

flare	here	bear
mere	pear	query
snare	declare	compare
hero	severe	glare
welfare	airline	zero
square	cereal	scare
sphere	share	atmosphere
wear	sincere	swear
dreary	nightmare	disappear
stare	experience	unaware

Make it

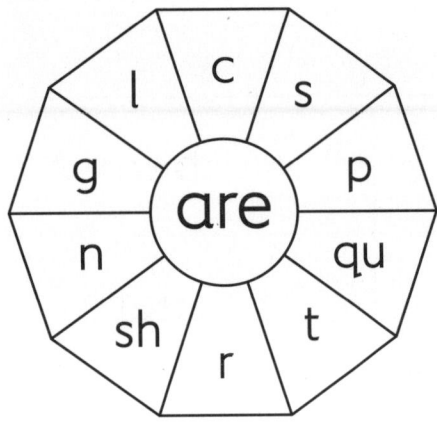 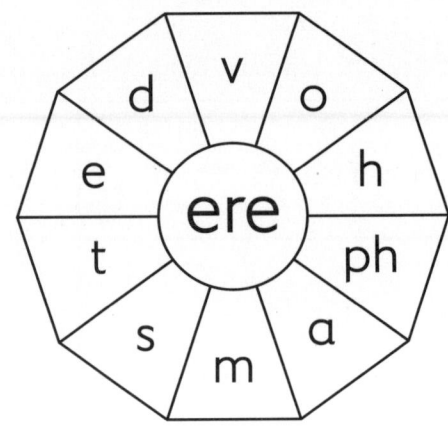

Hints:
1. To frighten.
2. A shape with four corners.
3. To split something in two and give someone else one part.

Hints:
1. In this exact spot.
2. Harsh.
3. A round 3D shape.

Session 14.1 /sh/ ti, ci

Map it

ore	o	y	a
ere	au	or	ear
u	ou	er	aw

Learn New Code

ti	ci
action	special
'ti' always appears in the middle of a word. It is often followed by 'on' or 'ous'.	'ci' always appears in the middle of a word. It is often followed by 'al' or 'an'.

Spell it: Add it

Word	Suffix	New Word	
infection	ious	infectious	3
ambition			
caution			
nutrition			
superstition			

Summary

ti		ci
action	superstition	special
relationship	infectious	politician
population	ambitious	artificial
infection	cautious	ancient
ambition	nutritious	
caution	superstitious	
nutrition		

Session 14.2 /sh/ ssi, si, su

Map it

e-e	are	y	ti
ee	ci	e	ie
ear	ea	air	sh

Learn New Code

ssi	**si**	**su**
passion	mansion	casual
'ssi' always appears in the middle of a word. It is usually followed by 'on'.	'si' always appears in the middle of a word. It is usually followed by 'on'.	'su' always appears in the middle of a word. It is usually followed by 'al' or 're'.

Spell it: Add it

Word	Suffix	New Word	
erode		erosion	3
conclude	ion		
explode			
decide			
divide			

Summary

ssi	si	su
passion expression percussion	mansion conclusion erosion division explosion decision	casual measure visual

Session 14.4

Code it

description	constellation	politician
fraction	precious	ancient
tension	controversial	mission
fiction	mansion	suspicion
facial	motion	discussion
social	optician	delicious
ration	expansion	dimension
depression	revulsion	extension
lotion	emotion	especially
magician	potion	comprehension

Make it

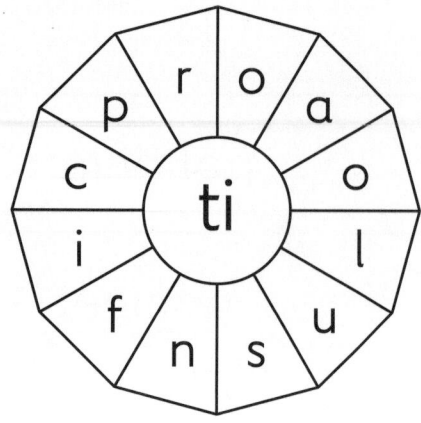

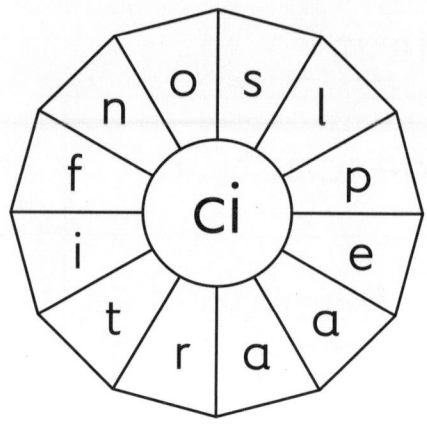

Hints:
1. A novel is a work of f_____.
2. A choice = o_____
3. A mixture made by a witch.

Hints:
1. You get your glasses from an o_____n.
2. Important to you = s_____
3. A party is a s_____ gathering.

Complete the Code Chart

Consonants

 /b/	 /c/	 /d/	 /f/	 /g/	 /h/	 /j/	 /l/	 /m/	 /n/
b	c	d	f	g	h	j	l	m	n
bb	k	dd	ff	gg		g	ll	mm	nn
	ck		ph			ge			kn
	cc					dge			

/p/	/r/	/s/	/t/	/v/	/w/	/x/	/y/	/z/
p	r	s	t	v	w	x	y	z
pp	rr	ss	tt		wh			zz
	wr	c						
		ce						
		sc						

Consonant Digraphs

 /ch/	 /ng/	 /nk/	 /qu/	 /sh/	 /th/
ch	ng	nk	qu	sh	th
tch				ti	
ture*				ssi	
				ci	
				si	
				/zh/ su	

*This has a slight schwa at the end, 'chuh'.

Glossary

blend: We blend phonemes together to make a word. For example, c-a-t is blended together to make the word 'cat'.

code it out loud: When we code a word out loud, we say each of the phonemes in the word. For example, the word 'cat' coded out is c-a-t.

digraph: Two letters that together make one phoneme (sound). For example, the digraph 'sh' makes the sound /sh/ in the word 'shot'.

grapheme: A letter, or group of letters, that represents a phoneme (sound). For example, the word 'cat' has three graphemes: 'c', 'a' and 't'.

phoneme: A sound within a word. For example, there are three phonemes in the word 'cat': /c/, /a/, /t/.

prefix: A group of letters we add to the start of a word to change its meaning. For example, 'rewrite' is 'write' with 're-' added at the beginning, so 're-' is the prefix.

schwa: An unstressed vowel sound that is in a lot of words. It sounds a bit like 'uh'. For example, in the word 'doctor', the second vowel sound is a schwa. In 'elephant', the final vowel sound is a schwa.

split digraph: A split digraph represents a vowel sound where its two letters are split by a consonant (for example, 'a-e' in 'take'). The two letters (here 'a' and 'e') count as one digraph, making one sound.

suffix: A group of letters we add to the end of a word to change its meaning. For example, 'playing' is 'play' + '-ing', so '-ing' is the suffix.

syllable: A beat of sound within a word. For example, the word 'sunset' has two syllables: 'sun' and 'set'.

tricky word: A common word that cannot be decoded easily because it contains one or more unusual graphemes. For example, in the word 'of', the grapheme 'f' makes the sound /v/.

trigraph: Three letters that together make one phoneme (sound). For example, the trigraph 'igh' makes the sound /igh/ in the word 'night'.

tweak it: When we tweak it, we slightly adjust how we say a word to make it sound right. For example, for 'doctor', we say 'doct-UH' not 'doct-OR'.

Vowels

 /a/ a	 /e/ e ea	 /i/ i y	 /o/ o a	 /u/ u o ou

Vowel Digraphs and Trigraphs

 /ai/ a-e ai ay a	 /air/ air are ear	 /ar/ ar	 /ear/ ear er ere	 /ee/ y ea ee e ie e-e	 /er/ er	 /igh/ igh i-e i y ie
 /oa/ ow o o-e oa	 /oi/ oi oy	 /oo/ /yoo/ oo u ew u-e ue	 /oo/ oo	 /or/ or a aw au ore	 /ow/ ou ow	 /ur/ er ur ir or